Work Sheets for
Identifying and Closing
Culture-Gaps

RALPH H. KILMANN
AND ASSOCIATES

Distributed by
KILMANN DIAGNOSTICS
1 Suprema Drive
Newport Coast, CA 92657
www.kilmanndiagnostics.com
info@kilmanndiagnostics.com
949.497.8766

WORK SHEETS ON

IDENTIFYING CULTURE-GAPS

Key Topics:
- Surfacing Actual Norms
- Establishing Desired Norms
- Pinpointing the Largest Culture-Gaps
- Designing a Sanctioning System
- Using Your Sanctioning System

RALPH H. KILMANN

Introduction

Every organization has its unwritten rules that significantly affect how people interact with one another and how the work gets done. Unwritten rules that prescribe how to get ahead, how to stay out of trouble, what the boss really wants, and how to treat other groups in the organization are simply treated as normal: "It's just the way we do things around here."

On the top half of each of the following pages, list the **actual norms** that are operating in your work group or department. The classic "Believe in External Control and Hope for the Best" is purposely listed first, but you have room to add fifteen more actual norms. For each one you list, your work group is asked to discuss how the implied behavior interferes with organizational success. Then, in the space provided on the lower half of each page, your work group should establish the **desired norms** that will improve its contribution to the whole organization. *Try to make these desired norms as behaviorally specific as possible—so that they can be monitored and enforced by your work group.*

Once you have surfaced the dysfunctional actual norms and established the desired norms, you will be requested to design a sanctioning system: a social mechanism for helping one another break the unconscious habit of enacting the outdated **actual norms** while encouraging the regular use of the newly established **desired norms**.

1A. Actual Norm:

Believe in External Control and Hope for the Best

There seems to be an underlying—collective—belief in external control: What happens to you (and your organization) is largely determined by *outside forces*—an underlying belief that you couldn't make a difference anyway, so why try? "You can't do that! Who said you could? It can't be done. What's the use of trying?" Why would you spend much time or effort attempting to improve your organization, if you already believe that what happens is largely determined by someone else?

1B. Desired Norm:

2A. Actual Norm:

2B. Desired Norm:

3A. Actual Norm:

3B. Desired Norm:

4A. Actual Norm:

_____
_____
_____
_____
_____
_____
_____

4B. Desired Norm:

_____
_____
_____
_____
_____
_____
_____
_____
_____
_____

5A. Actual Norm:

5B. Desired Norm:

6A. Actual Norm:

6B. Desired Norm:

7A. Actual Norm:

7B. Desired Norm:

8A. Actual Norm:

_____

_____

_____

_____

_____

_____

_____

8B. Desired Norm:

_____

_____

_____

_____

_____

_____

_____

_____

_____

_____

9A. Actual Norm:

9B. Desired Norm:

10A. Actual Norm:

10B. Desired Norm:

11A. Actual Norm

11B. Desired Norm:

12A. Actual Norm:

12B. Desired Norm:

13A. Actual Norm:

13B. Desired Norm:

14A. Actual Norm:

_____

_____

_____

_____

_____

_____

14B. Desired Norm:

_____

_____

_____

_____

_____

_____

_____

_____

15A. Actual Norm:

15B. Desired Norm:

16A. Actual Norm:

_____

_____

_____

_____

_____

_____

_____

16B. Desired Norm:

_____

_____

_____

_____

_____

_____

_____

_____

_____

_____

_____

Pinpointing the Largest Culture-Gaps

Now that your work group has established the desired norms that are essential to its effective functioning in the organization, please review the whole list to separate the largest culture-gaps from the smallest. For example, if you had to choose only five culture-gaps to concentrate all your efforts at cultural change, what would they be? If you find it easiest to list a slightly different number of gaps (such as six or eight), that is fine. But do try to zero in on the largest culture-gaps that require your special attention.

1. _____

2. _____

3. _____

4. _____

5. _____

6. _____

7. _____

8. _____

Designing a Sanctioning System

What positive or negative sanctions will be provided to group members when **victories** or **violations** occur in the workplace (enacting desired versus outdated cultural norms, respectively)? How will you help one another break the dysfunctional habits of the past and do all the things that are essential for achieving organizational success today?

Designing a Sanctioning System (Continued)

Using Your Sanctioning System

Members must break the *unconscious conspiracy:* "I won't bring it to your attention whenever you violate one of our desired norms if you promise to do the same for me." Keep in mind: Anyone who says he does not need a sanctioning system is actually saying, "I don't want to change and I don't want to be reminded of that fact either!"

How will your group ensure that the sanctioning system you developed is *used* as intended? Who will monitor and foster the use of the system on a daily basis?

WORK SHEETS ON
CLOSING CULTURE-GAPS

Key Topics:
- Calculate Group Culture-Gaps
- Identify Root Causes of Gaps
- Develop Solutions to Close Gaps
- Develop and Apply Action Plans to Close Gaps
- Monitor Progress and Reassess Gaps

Plus the All-Purpose Sanctioning System

RALPH H. KILMANN

1. Calculate Group Culture-Gaps

Ask every member in your work group to complete the *Kilmann-Saxton Culture-Gap® Survey* (Newport Coast, CA: Kilmann Diagnostics, 2011). Once all the people in your group have obtained their scores on the four culture-gaps, collect all these numbers together on a sheet of paper and calculate four gaps: a group average for Task Support, Task Innovation, Social Relationships, and Personal Freedom. While computing these four averages, be sure to divide the sum of the scores for each culture-gap by the right number of individuals in your work group: those who actually provided their scores for these calculations. Also, be sure to include the proper sign (+ or –) for each culture-gap score in all calculations. Lastly, place the averages in the spaces provided below and graph the results—as described on page 14 in the *Kilmann-Saxton Culture-Gap® Survey*:

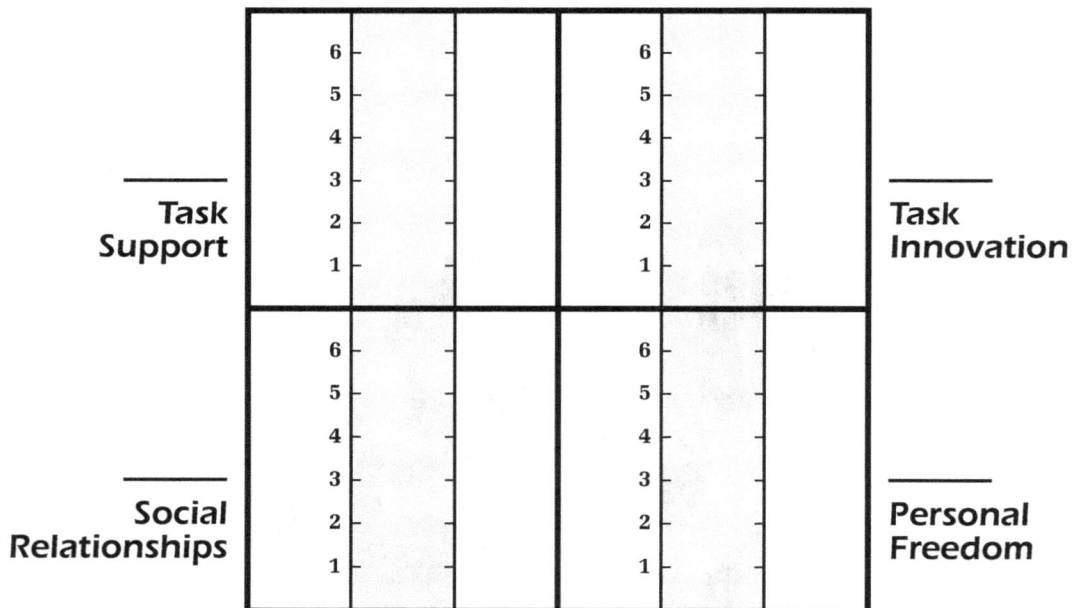

Task Support   **Task Innovation**

Social Relationships   **Personal Freedom**

Culture-Gap® Profile

2. Identify Root Causes of Gaps

For each of the four culture-gaps, discuss the root causes that create or reinforce the differences between actual and desired cultural norms—the reasons *why* each culture-gap exists. Concentrate on the specific causes that are under the *direct control* of your work group.

Recall that an average of +3 or more may represent a significant culture-gap for your group—as does any negative average (–2, for example). Any group score that is less than +3 should be examined to see if any group member has an individual score greater than +3. If so, even though the group average is not significant as such, it is apparent that at least one member does see a significant culture-gap operating in the group. The underlying causes of these different perceptions should be examined explicitly: Perhaps some members defined the same words differently when they responded to the survey; or maybe the rest of the group is denying or *avoiding* culture-gaps that at least one member is willing to acknowledge openly.

2. Identify Root Causes of Gaps (Continued)

3. Develop Solutions to Close Gaps

For each culture-gap that poses significant barriers to your organization's success, derive solutions that you believe will, if implemented properly, close the gap between actual and desired cultural norms (or at least bring it within an acceptable range: less than +3 for every member in the work group). *Please be sure to concentrate on those solutions that your group can implement on the job.* Do not prescribe solutions for other groups or departments in the organization.

4. Develop and Apply Action Plans to Close Gaps

For each solution to a culture-gap that you derived in the previous step, develop a specific action plan (including people, tasks, responsibilities, and deadlines) for effectively implementing your solution back on the job. Be sure to develop action plans and schedules that are reasonable and realistic—given time constraints and resource limitations. Then, of course, you must apply your action plans to close all your culture-gaps!

5. Monitor Progress and Reassess Gaps

How will your group assess if its action plans are being implemented as intended? How will your group handle any unanticipated events that negatively affect its plans? What signals will be used to convince your group that its gaps have been brought within an acceptable range?

Plus the All-Purpose Sanctioning System

Can your group expand the design and use of its sanctioning system to close its largest culture-gaps? How will your group confront its members when they enact the outdated norms (a violation)? How will your group congratulate its members when they act according to the desired norms (a victory)?

Assessment Tools for the Eight Tracks
Distributed by Kilmann Diagnostics

Kilmann-Saxton Culture-Gap® Survey

Kilmanns Organizational Belief Survey

Kilmanns Time-Gap Survey

Kilmanns Team-Gap Survey

Organizational Courage Assessment

Kilmann-Covin Organizational Influence Survey

Plus the Online Version of the

Thomas-Kilmann Conflict Mode Instrument

www.ingramcontent.com/pod-product-compliance
Lightning Source LLC
Chambersburg PA
CBHW081205270326
41930CB00014B/3306